D0594699

PRESENTED BY AND WITH

MAXWELL
& WILLIAMS
DESIGNER HOMEWARES

TABLE TRICKS

Presented by and with Maxwell & Williams Designer Homewares Deutschland GmbH, Marsberg

Copyright © Brand Expression GmbH, Hamburg

Concept and design: Brand Expression GmbH, Hamburg
Photography: Uli Kohl, Berlin (food), Alexander Rieder, Vienna
(food styling), Andreas Hoffmannbeck, Münster (people),
produced in the Brand Expression studio, Münster

Special thanks to Laura von Deuten, Uli Kohl, Jessica
Stade and Lisa Große Kleimann, without whose efforts
this book would not have been such a success.

ISBN 978-3-00-024722-4

This is not a cookery book!

Every one of us eats and drinks, some of us too much, others too little. Many of us watch cookery shows on television and buy cookery books, but only a few of us bother to spend time actually cooking in the kitchen – a sign of the times.

This book focuses on the reality between our daily job, shopping for groceries and inviting people home for a treat. As the title 'Table Tricks' suggests, it provides simple tips for adding that special sparkle to our food.

After all, well presented food simply tastes better, irrespective of whether the recipe stems from Grandma's folder or whether, as is often the case nowadays, shopped for in the local supermarket or delicatessen. In both cases table presentation is the name of the game!

This guide is intentionally full of photos and brief descriptions to inspire you to get out there, follow your own tastebuds and shopping list, and add that little extra zest to the ingredients.

Once you have finished reading this book you will be pleasantly surprised at just how simple it was to make a good impression, and your guests will be impressed.

Just enjoy!

ps: special thanks go to Maxwell & Williams - all photos show porcelain or fine bone china, cutlery, glasses or accessories from Maxwell & Williams.

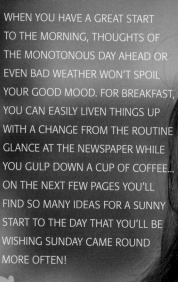

WHEN YOU HAVE A GREAT START TO THE MORNING, THOUGHTS OF THE MONOTONOUS DAY AHEAD OR EVEN BAD WEATHER WON'T SPOIL YOUR GOOD MOOD. FOR BREAKFAST, YOU CAN EASILY LIVEN THINGS UP WITH A CHANGE FROM THE ROUTINE GLANCE AT THE NEWSPAPER WHILE YOU GULP DOWN A CUP OF COFFEE... ON THE NEXT FEW PAGES YOU'LL FIND SO MANY IDEAS FOR A SUNNY START TO THE DAY THAT YOU'LL BE WISHING SUNDAY CAME ROUND MORE OFTEN!

Sunny start to the day

From breakfast, to brunch, to teatime and beyond!

A healthy mix

EVERYONE KNOWS WHAT MAKES A HEALTHY BREAKFAST: FRUIT,
GRAINS AND MUESLI KEEP YOU FIT AND ALERT, REPLENISH ENER-
GY STORES IN A FLASH AND STRENGTHEN THE IMMUNE SYSTEM.
BUT WHEN THE DULL, DRY FLAKES COME POURING OUT OF THE
PACKET, IT SOMEHOW DOESN'T SEEM QUITE SO APPEALING. WHY
NOT TRY MIXING UP SOMETHING NEW EVERY MORNING TO SUIT
YOUR MOOD USING DIFFERENT INGREDIENTS? GIVE YOURSELF A
GREAT START TO THE DAY!

Apples, berries,
dried fruit
A mini fruit buffet

With this refreshing treat, everyone puts together their own fruit salad. Seasonal fruit, brought to the table fresh from the market, conjures up a whole array of fruity aromas. Serve in a few separate dishes, drizzled with a touch of honey or lemon juice, or sprinkled with a few chopped nuts or chocolate shavings – pure natural ingredients have never tasted so delicious...

TABLE Tricks

Muesli fans can join in the breakfast jigsaw fun too: serve all the ingredients separately so that everyone can create their own favourite mixture. It looks so good and tastes even better! Who knows, you might even invent some new combinations - marmalade and pine kernels... or vanilla yoghurt with kiwi... Delicious!

sunny and
fresh

Fresh breakfast fun

CHIC MOZZARELLA BALLS AND EVERYDAY QUARK ARE DISTANT RELATIVES –
REASON ENOUGH TO TAKE ADVANTAGE OF THEIR SIMILARITIES. THIS DISH
APPEALS TO THE EYE AS WELL AS TO THE TASTEBUDS – SET THEM TINGLING
WITH THE FLAVOUR AND FRESHNESS HIDING IN THESE LITTLE BALLS...

Quark balls

Before you start: the whey must be drained from the quark to make it easier to mould. Simply squeeze it out through a clean tea towel...

...then use an ice cream scoop or a melon scoop, two spoons or your fingers to mould the quark solids into little balls...

For experts

Preparation
approx. 45 mins

...roll them in the chopped herbs, spices, nuts or chocolate shavings
you have prepared and cover them on all sides, tap them into shape
and they're ready!

For instant sophistication, you could fill the balls as you mould them.
How about a little olive? Or a strawberry? Whatever takes your fancy!

Inspiration

Looking for a little dish of inspiration? Of course, as every child learns, you shouldn't play with your food, but a playful approach to treats at the table is definitely allowed – if it looks good enough to eat, it tastes even better!

Egg surprises

THE 5-MINUTE EGG, OFTEN COOKED FIFTY MINUTES IN ADVANCE, IS A FIRM FAVOURITE AT THE BREAKFAST TABLE. BUT THERE ARE BETTER AND OFTEN EVEN EASIER WAYS TO SERVE AN EGG THAN BOILING IT TILL IT ROLLS AROUND AND EXPLODES OUT OF ITS SHELL! HOW DO YOU FANCY FRIED EGG 'IN' TOAST? A REAL SURPRISE BUT EASY TO MAKE AND READY IN MINUTES...

Fried egg 'in' toast

Easy

Preparation
approx. 15 mins
+ toasting time

2

1

Carefully press a perfectly round
hole out of each slice of toast
using an upturned glass...

...leaving enough toast round
the edges to make sure it stays
intact...

...cook to your taste, turn over if you wish, and it's ready to serve!

4

...place in a hot buttered frying pan, and pour the egg into the round hole...

3

TABLE Tricks

Even the classics can be turned into a special treat when you pay attention to the presentation. A boiled egg on a bed of salt will stay warm longer, and besides, it looks lovely and doesn't wobble! Bacon rashers grilled on greaseproof paper in the oven, and dabbed with kitchen roll make a crunchy addition to the perfect breakfast. Or you could roll them up and fill them with cream cheese. Serve scrambled eggs with boiled tomatoes to complete the look and enhance the flavour. Why not use porcelain serving plates to give each little delicacy its own place?

Sunny start to the day | 31

WHY NOT USE AN ESPRESSO CUP AS A CAKE MOULD?
FRESHLY BAKED MUFFINS OR EVEN TRADITIONAL MARBLE
CAKE MAKE AN ATTRACTIVE SIGHT IN THESE LITTLE
CUPS - AT BREAKFAST, BRUNCH OR EVEN DESSERT THEY
ARE SIMPLY IRRESISTIBLE. JUST PREPARE THE CAKE MIX
AS NORMAL, WHETHER YOU'RE FOLLOW-
ING GRANDMA'S RECIPE OR USING
READY-MADE CAKE MIX, THEN
FILL UP THE CUP, POP IN THE
OVEN, AND BRING THESE
MOREISH MUFFINS TO
THE TABLE FOR YOUR
HUNGRY GUESTS.

Espresso
cup cakes

Choc-nut muffins in espresso cups

...and fill them with cake mix. Impotant: do not fill them up to the rim, the cakes will rise...

Prepare the cake mix as normal. Grease the cups...

For 'Choc-nut muffin' recipe see pg. 185

3

Easy

Preparation
approx. 15 mins
+ baking time

...sprinkle with chocolate chips or
chopped nuts...

4

...pop them straight in the oven and serve
warm with a saucer underneath. Don't they
look fantastic?

TABLE
Tricks

Milky coffee, latte, café au lait ... the principle's the same whether you're at home or in one of Paris' famous coffee houses! Why not mix it yourself? Serve the coffee and hot milk separately in little jugs. They not only look attractive, but the coffee and milk stay hot for longer in pre-heated jugs and everyone can mix the perfect coffee according to their taste...if you like, you could even mix in a drop of vanilla or caramel syrup. There are no limits to the sweet and creamy combinations!

Quick light bites and snacks

LIGHT LUNCH

SOMETIMES YOU DON'T HAVE TIME OR AREN'T HUNGRY ENOUGH FOR A BIG MEAL, BUT YOU STILL WANT TO ENJOY YOUR FOOD. WHETHER YOU'RE IN A BUSINESS MEETING OR CATCHING UP WITH A FRIEND, A TASTY SNACK OR A GLASS OF WINE HELPS YOU DISCOVER THINGS IN COMMON AND KEEPS CONVERSATION FLOWING. YOU'LL FIND SOME DELICIOUS IDEAS ON THE NEXT FEW PAGES.

Tramezzini toastie bites

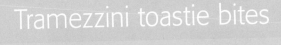

Super soups

Pasta con bellezza

Beetroot, radish and potato puree towers

TRAMEZZINI
TOASTIE
BITES

TRADITIONAL YET INFAMOUS, THE MEAT-FILLED SANDWICH PLATTER IS STUFFED
WITH FILLINGS PROBABLY MORE SUITED TO THE APPETITES OF A GROUP OF STEEL
WORKERS THAN TODAY'S BRAINSTORMERS AND TEAM PLAYERS, WHOSE CALORIE
NEEDS ONLY STRETCH TO MOUSE CLICKS RATHER THAN A DAY'S HARD LABOUR!
HOWEVER, WITH A FEW TRICKS UP YOUR SLEEVE, YOU CAN EASILY CREATE LIGHT
AND APPEALING BITES. AS ALWAYS, YOU CAN USE YOUR TASTES AND IMAGINATION
TO DECIDE WHAT TO PUT INSIDE! ENJOY!

Multi-storey sandwich

See pp. 186 for filling suggestions

Easy

Preparation
approx. 15 mins.
+ ingredients

Toast slices of a variety of breads,
removing the dark, hard crusts.

Cut the slices of toast into manageable, bite-
size quarters and fill with your choice of filling. Use
herbs or radishes to add colour and vibrancy.

3

Alternate the fillings and stack according to your taste. If necessary, use a cocktail stick to secure the sandwiches. To make the edges attractive, butter one edge of the sandwiches and sprinkle on some finely chopped herbs.

ps. if you're feeling adventurous, you could cut the slices of bread lengthways to make them even thinner!

TABLE
TRICKS

This is a particularly pretty example of the multi-storey sandwich, fanned out attractively, just to show what's possible. Use thin slices of bread as a basis, then add different spreads to give flavour and to stick the slices together, and fill with an imaginative mixture of ham and different varieties of lettuce. The principle always remains the same, even if the possible fillings are limitless. How about a vegetarian toastie filled with delicious vegetables? Egg and bacon? Roast beef, apple horseradish and beetroot? Only gravity sets the limits – the more storeys you stack up, the bigger the challenge to keep it from falling down!

SOUPS ARE QUICK TO PREPARE, QUICK TO SERVE AND QUICK TO EAT, WHICH IS WHAT MAKES THEM SUCH A POPULAR CHOICE FOR A STARTER OR A SMALL SNACK. WHETHER IT'S HOME-MADE FROM A TRADITIONAL RECIPE OR GRABBED FROM THE SUPERMARKET SHELF TO FIT IN WITH YOUR BUSY LIFESTYLE, YOU CAN ADD GLAMOUR TO EVERY SOUP WITH A FEW LITTLE TRICKS. FOR EXAMPLE, WHY SHOULD SOUP ALWAYS BE SERVED ON ITS OWN? SERVED IN LITTLE DISHES – OR EVEN ESPRESSO CUPS – A CHOICE OF SOUPS OFFERS AN ATTRACTIVE VARIETY. SERVE ANOTHER LITTLE NIBBLE WITH IT, AND EVEN THE SIMPLEST SOUP BECOMES A CULINARY MASTERPIECE!

SUPER
SOUPS

Whipped-up herby soup

A good stock provides the basis for this soup (meat, fish or poultry, preferably home-made but you can also use a jar. In an emergency, stock cubes or granules will do), thickened with cream or crème fraîche and reduced down a little...

You can add flavour and colour to the soup with powerful herbs such as watercress, sorrel or even basil or a mixture of different herbs (just experiment!). Alternatively, you could combine chestnuts and apple, carrot and ginger... let your imagination run wild!

Easy

Preparation
approx. 20 mins.
+ stock

For 'Whipped-up herby soup' recipe, see pg. 189

Mix up the soup using a hand-held blender. With a bit of luck and
some more heat from the stove, the flavours and colours will emerge
to bring the soup to life and transform it into a frothy delight.

TABLE
TRICKS

There is such a large variety of soups – the expert divides them into crèmes, consommés, véloutes and potages – and there is also a huge variety of ways to serve them. Go for classical style and ladle it into a large soup bowl, or pour elegantly into a dish which sits on a plate, with room for bread or other accompaniments. Or perhaps something more unusual – serve it in a cup or a glass (this looks especially attractive when serving bright-coloured soups), or in a soufflé dish topped with cheese. All you need here is a bit of creative flair – you could even serve it in bottles! Great for a reception or finger buffet, it certainly attracts attention whatever the occasion! The humble soup finally makes it big!

PASTA
CON
BELLEZZA

THE CORNERSTONE OF ITALIAN CUISINE, PASTA WAS NOT EVEN INVENTED THERE, BUT WAS A HINT AT WHAT TODAY'S GLOBALISED WORLD WOULD BECOME. MARCO POLO BROUGHT NOODLES BACK TO ITALY FROM THE FAR EAST, AND FROM THERE IT BEGAN TO PROCLAIM ITS VICTORY MARCH AND CONQUERED THE WORLD! TODAY, IT HAS BECOME BRITAIN'S FAVOURITE READY-MEAL – TINNED RAVIOLI HAS BEEN THE BEST-SELLING CONVENIENCE FOOD FOR DECADES. BUT THERE ARE OTHER WAYS OF DOING IT, AS THE FOLLOWING PAGES SHOW...

Prawns on a pasta nest

Make sure you warm the plates! Then take the cooked pasta – long varieties such as spaghetti, tagliatelle, linguine, fettuccine, pappardelle or cappellini work best – out of the water with tongs or a fork and allow the water to drain briefly...

Whether you choose prawns, seafood or something entirely different, served on a nest of pasta these ingredients will immediately ennoble any pasta dish....

ps: for extra decoration, serve with little dishes of suitable accompaniments such as tomato sauce, chopped chillies and freshly grated cheese. Every one can try what they like and serve up their own portions – even more fun at the dinner table!

...and arrange the pasta in the shape of nests on the hot plates. Place the topping inside the nest, sprinkle over herbs and spices and serve immediately.

Easy

Preparation
approx. 20 mins.

For 'Prawns on a pasta nest' recipe, see p. 190

Springtime pasta

Pipette, rigatoni, tubetti or tufoli – whatever they're called, for this recipe you need short pasta tubes with a large diameter, so the delicious fillings point up to the sky!

For 'Springtime pasta' recipe, see pg. 59

Easy

Preparation
approx. 25 mins.
+ fillings and sauces

1

2

Arrange the fresh pasta (pre-cook if necessary) upright in ovenproof dishes and fill with bolognaise sauce, vegetables or sugo according to your tastes. You can even fill them with different fillings to make the dish more interesting!

3

Fill up the dishes with a sauce that goes with all the fillings (e.g. tomato, cheese or herb sauce). If you like, you could sprinkle on some grated cheese and brown in the oven.

TABLE
TRICKS

Even nowadays no one knows just how many varieties of pasta there really are. Every region, every city, every area of Italy boasts with pride about the unique characteristics of the local pasta, which is beyond comparison with any other - reason enough to make the most of this variety in the kitchen. There are thousands of imaginative variations on the 'pasta in sauce' principle. Why not use orecchiette (which means 'little ears') or fill others such as lumache (snails) with sugo, then pour over a sauce and cover with cheese on the plate... buon apetito!

FLASH-FRIED with VEGETABLE TOWERS

YOU DON'T HAVE TO GO WITHOUT A PIECE OF FISH OR MEAT WHEN PLANNING A LIGHT MEAL. HAVE SOME FRESHLY FILLETED BY YOUR FISH-MONGER OR BUTCHER, THEN PUT IT STRAIGHT INTO A PAN OR UNDER THE GRILL – IT'S QUICK TO MAKE AND KEEPS ITS FLAVOUR AND NUTRI-ENTS. IF YOU SERVE IT WITH ELEGANTLY PRESENTED VEGETABLES AND SIDE DISHES, YOU NEED NOT FEEL LIKE SOMETHING'S MISSING JUST BE-CAUSE THERE'S NO HEAVY SAUCE – HOW ABOUT A LITTLE TOWER, EASILY MADE WITH A PASTRY RING.

Beetroot, radish and puree towers

Grease a pastry ring (you can buy these or make
your own from small, flat empty tins, by removing
the top and bottom with a tin opener) – this
is what will serve as a mould for the tower.

Take the pre-cooked and finely sliced beetroot and radish
(you can also use other vegetables if you wish) and
lay them around the inside of the pastry ring.

Fill with potato puree.

Keep warm and carefully remove the ring before serving – the impressive masterpiece is finished!

The technique used for this dish can be used to serve a whole host of different side dishes – lamb's lettuce with potato? Red cabbage with apple? Just experiment with something new!

TABLE
TRICKS

The 'light lunch' motif can also be a feature of the table decoration. Sticking to light colours and simple place mats doesn't mean your table can't be stylish. When you're having something quick to eat, the decoration can be more understated – just snip something colourful from the garden for each guest or take a few flowers from the bouquet they've brought along, and you'll soon bring an atmosphere of freshness to the table. Unpretentious crockery and glasses in contemporary designs are nice when there's no big occasion, and when combined with thoughtful touches, they make a great impression. Enjoy!

LOTS OF IDEAS, MINIMAL WORK, HAPPY GUESTS

AN EVENING WITH FRIENDS IS DEFINITELY SOMETHING
TO LOOK FORWARD TO, BUT IT ALWAYS COMES BACK
TO THAT OLD DILEMMA – DO YOU SLAVE AWAY IN
THE KITCHEN ALONE PLAYING WAITER AND MISS ALL
THE FUN? OR JUST RING FOR A PIZZA AND SERVE IT
STRAIGHT OUT OF THE CARDBOARD BOX? HERE YOU'LL
FIND PLENTY OF IDEAS THAT WILL BRING YOUR GUESTS
BACK FOR MORE, BUT DON'T NEED A LOT OF WORK.
ENJOY!

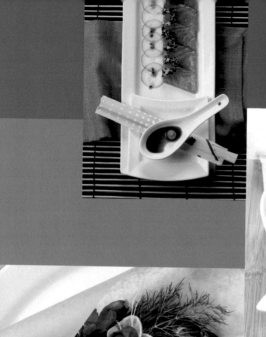

Asia-style starter 72

Stuffed vegetables 78

Fish parcel 84

Fruit strudel 90

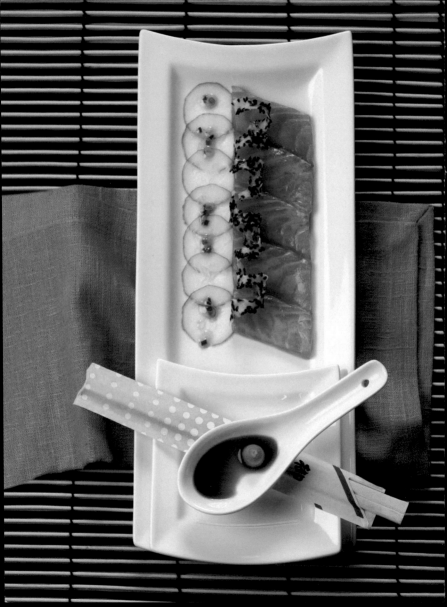

Asia

-STYLE

Starter

SUSHI & CO. ARE ALWAYS UNDERRATED FOR HOME COOKING – WE
EITHER HAVE IT DELIVERED BY THE PROFESSIONALS OR WE GET OUR
TRUSTED FISHMONGER TO SLICE THE BEST FILLETS. AS WELL AS
UNCOMPROMISING QUALITY AND FRESHNESS, SUSHI ALWAYS LOOKS
VERY DECORATIVE WITH THINLY SLICED VEGETABLES, CAREFULLY
PREPARED SAUCES FOR DIPPING OR THE LEGENDARY SESAME CURL. THE
SECRET IS THAT EVERYTHING CAN BE PREPARED IN ADVANCE, STRESS
FREE, AND CAN BE TAKEN OUT OF THE FRIDGE READY TO SERVE IN NO
TIME... LET'S DO IT!

SESAME CURL

For 'Sesame curl' recipe, see pg. 196

For experts

Preparation approx. 45 mins.

2 ...take the pastry snake, which shou still be flexible, and, leaving it in the paper, wrap carefully around a long wooden spoon handle,..

1 It's definitely worth the effort! Pipe out some pastry in a wiggly line on a piece of greaseproof paper covered with black sesame seeds. Bake briefly in the oven...

4 Carefully remove the spoon from the paper and gently ease the finished sesame curl off the handle. Now isn't that a sight to behold!

3 ...put it back in the oven to bake through until crisp and golden. Leave to cool.

TABLE
Tricks

You can easily create Asian style
in your own home. Chopsticks
are a must (more than 2 billion
people can't be wrong!) and
guarantee an authentic delight
and lots of fun trying them
out! Bamboo tablemats or
minimalist decorations will be
sure to set minds wandering to
the Far East...

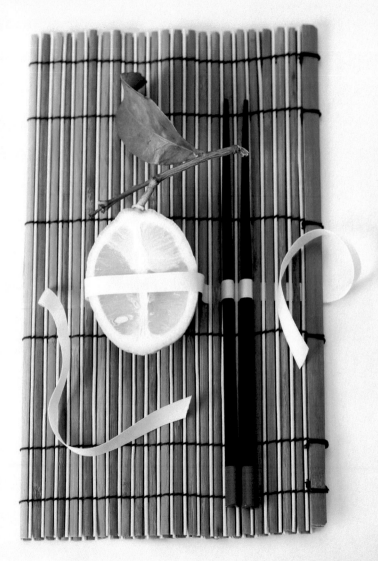

Stuffed VEGETABLES

THE PRETTIEST CONTAINERS CAN ONLY BE FOUND GROWING IN NATURE'S GARDEN – YOU JUST HAVE TO HOLLOW THEM OUT! THEY PROMISE TO CAPTIVATE WITH THEIR DELICATE FLAVOUR – IN THIS RECIPE, THE SERVING SUGGESTION IS PART OF THE DISH ITSELF! FROM A FOR AUBERGINE TO Z FOR ZUCCHINI, THE CHOICE IS ENDLESS, AND THE POSSIBLE FILLINGS ARE JUST AS VARIED! HOW ABOUT A RUSTIC RAGOUT? OR RISOTTO? SEAFOOD IN COCKTAIL SAUCE? WHATEVER YOUR TASTES, THESE ATTRACTIVE DISHES WILL APPEAL TO EVERYONE...

ZIG ZAG ZUCCHINI

For 'Zig zag

1 Cut open the zucchini in a zig-zag, leaving a larger portion at the bottom for the filling...

...remove the flesh from the bottom half, and keep it to one side for the filling if liked...

2

3

...stuff the empty half with your choice filling and either cook in the oven or sauté, depending on the filling. Cook the top half briefly as well, and put on top as a lid shortly before serving...

ps: Want to spend more time with your guests? Prepare the stuffed vegetables in advance and put them in the oven shortly before the meal.

TABLE
Tricks

The vegetable garden provides lots of other treats for the eye, but they're at their best when the little bundles of goodness look as if they're fresh out of the ground. The classic is the carrot, which keeps its shape when peeled carefully and its green head has been trimmed down to bite size. Bunches of radishes should have their leaves left on to serve, as should, for example, zucchini flowers or kohlrabi. For vegetables which don't come with their own greenery, you can easily dress them up to look the part – just arrange some fresh herbs like flat leaf parsley or basil on their stems. A strip of cooking twine holds everything together and looks a picture.

Fish
PARCEL

THE THOUGHT OF COOKING FRESH FISH PUTS AS MUCH FEAR INTO SOME PEOPLE
AS FINDING A HUGE SHARK IN THE BATH TUB! BUT THANKFULLY, THIS DOES NOT
HAPPEN OFTEN, AND WITH THIS RECIPE, SERVING FISH NEED NOT BE SO TERRIFYING!
IT'S SIMPLE – JUST WRAP THE WHOLE FISH IN THE PAPER WITH A FEW SEASONINGS
AND HERBS, ADD A DROP OF OIL AND A SPLASH OF WINE, PACKAGE IT UP AND POP
IT IN THE OVEN. AND THAT'S IT – EVERYTHING ELSE TAKES CARE OF ITSELF. WHEN IT'S
COOKED, PUT IT STRAIGHT ONTO THE PLATES AND UNWRAP – DELICIOUS. IT'S UP TO
YOU WHETHER YOU USE SEA BREAM, SEA BASS OR SOLE – YOU CAN FOLLOW THE
FISHMONGER'S RECOMMENDATIONS OR TRY THEM OUT FOR YOURSELF. THE SAME
GOES FOR THE SEASONING – JUST FOLLOW YOUR TASTEBUDS!

SEA BREAM PARCEL

2

...to ensure it doesn't dry out. Wrap the paper tightly round the fish and close securely in a package to ensure as little steam escapes as possible, so the fish can cook in its own juice, and even creates its own sauce for serving.

1

Lightly oil some greaseproof paper, take your freshly washed fish and lay it on the paper with herbs and spices of your choice. You could even fill the belly with some onions and lemon. Whatever you choose, add a good splash of wine to send the fish on its final journey...

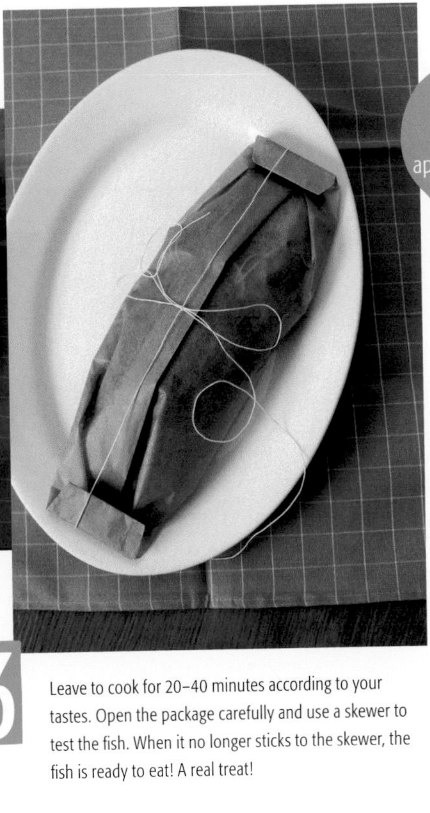

For 'Sea bream parcel' recipe, see pg. 199

Easy

Preparation
approx. 40-60 mins.

3 Leave to cook for 20–40 minutes according to your
tastes. Open the package carefully and use a skewer to
test the fish. When it no longer sticks to the skewer, the
fish is ready to eat! A real treat!

TABLE Tricks

Nobel Prize ceremony or wedding – there aren't many occasions which call for a formal dinner. With no dinner partners or dates, the occasion can be much less formal – why shouldn't everyone choose their own place at the table? Do it buffet-style rather than making a formal seating plan, and the same goes for the crockery and glasses. Everyone takes what they need and sits where they like. For each course, the guests re-group informally, the conversation flows! And the food still tastes great!

FRUIT STRUDEL

AGAIN IT'S NATURE'S BOUNTY WHICH PROVIDES THE INSPIRATION FOR THIS DISH – NESTLED ON A LITTLE BED OF PUFF PASTRY AND BAKED BRIEFLY, A WHOLE HOST OF FRUITS CAN BE DISPLAYED AT THEIR BEST AND MOST DELICIOUS. YOU CAN EITHER SERVE THEM STEAMING STRAIGHT FROM THE OVEN OR PREPARE THEM IN ADVANCE AND TAKE THEM OUT OF THE FRIDGE AS A REFRESHING TREAT. YET AGAIN, THERE ARE NO LIMITS TO THE IMAGINATION – APPLES WITH WALNUTS, PEARS WITH CHOCOLATE, TOPPED WITH YOUR CHOICE OF SAUCE... AN EASY AND SATISFYING END TO THE PERFECT EVENING WITH FRIENDS!

Slice the apples, being careful not to slice all the way through, then fan out the slices (as shown). In this way the apples will keep their shape better when baked in the oven.

Divide the pastry (pastry mix or from Grandma's recipe book) into the number of portions required and lay it on the greased oven dish. Peel and core the apples (leaving the stalk), then cut them in half. Drizzle a little lemon juice over the apples to stop them from discolouring.

For 'Apple tart' recipe, see pg. 200

Easy

Preparation approx. 30-40 mins.

3

Paint the pastry with the Calvados and egg yolk mixture. You can also add a few chopped nuts or raisins. Put the tarts in the oven. When they are ready, leave them in their dishes to serve. Mmmm...

TABLE Tricks

The butler says the pantry cook is ill? Then you'll have to use what you can find in the cupboards to decorate the table. It's easy – a jug becomes a vase, a glass becomes a lantern, a cup becomes a flowerpot. Stacks of plates and saucers create an impressive skyline – and why not? It's a shame all this beautiful porcelain only serves one purpose!

The best thing is that most pieces go well together, and if not, be daring – contrast just makes the arrangement even more interesting!

Happy Hour

Cocktails, APERITIFS AND SHAKES

THERE ARE SOME THINGS WHICH JUST CAN'T BE IMPROVED: SIPPING A BEER FROM THE CAN BY THE CAMPFIRE, GULPING DOWN WATER FROM THE PLASTIC BOTTLE WHEN YOU'RE RUNNING A 20 MILE MARATHON... BUT ON MOST OCCASIONS A BIT OF ADDED GLAMOUR WOULDN'T GO AMISS, WHETHER YOU'RE CELEBRATING YOUR FIRST DAY IN A NEW OFFICE, HAVING AN APERITIF BEFORE DINNER OR PLANNING A GARDEN PARTY... LUXURIOUS PRESENTATION WILL SET THE GLASSES CLINKING...

MARIE

Cocktail chic

Fresh
and fruity

Sparkling surprises

Cocktail chic

ENTER THE REALM OF THE DEMI-GODS IN WHITE, THOSE DIVINE
CREATURES PERFORMING MIRACLES BEHIND THE BAR. THEY
KNOW HOW TO TURN DRINKS INTO WORKS OF ART WHICH
TASTE AND LOOK DIVINE, AND, JUST AS IMPORTANT IN THE
BAR INDUSTRY, CREATE A TANTALISING DESCRIPTION FOR THE
MENU. A FEW OF THEIR TRICKS CAN ALSO BE PERFORMED
BEFORE MIDNIGHT AND AREN'T LIMITED TO DRINKS CONTAINING
STRONG SPIRITS – A FEW PIECES OF FRUIT, A SHOT OF SYRUP, A
COLOURFUL RIM – EVEN SIMPLE MINERAL WATER (OR ANY OTHER
DRINK) BECOMES AN EXPERIENCE! CHEERS!

Sweet sugar-rimmed glass

Easy

Preparation
approx. 10 mins.

Pour coloured sugar (from
a delicatessen) or a mixture
of sugar and coloured
beads onto a plate...

...moisten the rims of the
ses with some lemon juic
(you can also use water)..

...dip the glass in the sugar mixture straightaway...

...and the sugared rim is finished! Kids especially will love this colourful treat.

ps: If you use a heavier decoration (i.e. chocolate shavings instead of sugar), it needs to be stuck on more securely (i.e. use melted chocolate instead of lemon juice). Let the fun begin! A sturdier, non-breakable glass is better for children.

TABLE Tricks

Juice and water bottles, or even drinks cartons shouldn't be allowed at the table – jugs or carafes look much better and stay cool longer, especially if they're chilled before they're brought to the table. Add a handful of ice, slices of lemon, lime or orange, maybe even a few appropriate herbs such as mint or lemon balm – a refreshing way to present even the simplest of drinks.

Fresh
and fruity

PRACTICALLY A SMALL MEAL IN THEMSELVES, A SHAKE OR A SMOOTHIE MAKES THE PERFECT ALTERNATIVE TO DESSERT OR A SNACK BETWEEN MEALS, ESPECIALLY IN THE SUMMER. START WITH THE BASIC INGREDIENTS – MILK, BUTTERMILK, YOGHURT OR JUICE – ADD ICE FROM THE FREEZER AND A DASH OF FLAVOUR AND SWEETNESS WITH SYRUP OR LIQUEUR – WHATEVER YOU FANCY. THE PRINCIPLE IS THE SAME HERE AS ALWAYS – IF IT TASTES GOOD, IT'S ALLOWED, AND THE BEST COMBINATIONS PROBABLY HAVEN'T EVEN BEEN DISCOVERED YET! HAPPY MIXING, AND DON'T FORGET THE PRESENTATION – ICE BUCKET INSTEAD OF A TRAY, A FRUIT SKEWER FOR DECORATION...

Melon ball skewer

Using a small scoop, scoop out the flesh in little balls.

Take some ripe melon – you can use other fruit such as mango and papaya instead if you wish – in different colours and cut in half.

For fresh and fruity recipes, see pg. 200

3 Thread them onto a wooden skewer
with fresh herbs such as mint or lemon balm, and serve with the cocktails
or balance on the rim of the glass.

TABLE Tricks

Even child-friendly beakers should have some decoration. What about writing names around the outside, so that at a big party no one loses their cup or their place? Stickers written in wax crayon will last the evening but can easily be washed off. Add a few pieces of fruit, cut into slices and placed over the rim of the cup, or a colour-coordinated fruit skewer and you can guarantee that even choosing a drink will be a big event! PS. Not just for children, this treat is great for big kids, too!

Sparkling
surprises

EXPERTS WORRY THAT CHAMPAGNE PRODUCTION WILL SOON SPREAD TO
ENGLAND OR ROMANIA, OR EVEN IN DISTANT CHINA TO COPE WITH THE
RAPIDLY INCREASING DEMAND FOR LUXURIOUS SPARKLING WINE, EVEN
WITHOUT PROOF OF ORIGIN. AND THERE ARE PLENTY OF INVENTIVE IDEAS
FOR SERVING UP BUBBLY TREATS. HERE, TOO, FRUITY COLOURS AND TASTES
TAKE CENTRE STAGE, AS GUISEPPE OPRIANI REALISED WHEN HE CREATED
THE LEGENDARY BELLINI WITH A SIMPLE PROSECCO AND WHITE PEACHES,
WHICH SOON BECAME ONE OF THE MOST LUXURIOUS OF COCKTAILS.

Bellini

1

...then top up carefully with ice cold Prosecco poured over a spoon. How do you like it? Shaken or stirred, or just as it is?

2

Take some ripe peaches, preferably white, and peel them, remove the stone and puree them. If necessary, add some liqueur to help bring out the sun-ripened taste (careful – this betrays the northern European!). Dilute the peach puree with a few dashes of Prosecco and leave to chill. Pour into glasses...

Easy

Preparation approx. 30 mins.

For 'Bellini' recipe see pg. 202

3

In Cipriani's legendary Harry's Bar the Bellini is always served stirred, but the unmixed version looks even more attractive – just imagine the sun setting over the Giudecca…

The best champagnes are often smashed against the sides of ships at their launching ceremonies or sprayed over top sportsmen, especially on the Formula 1 circuit... but how should a top-quality sparkling wine really be served? Firstly, the chilled bottle is opened, either with a decisive stroke of the sabre

(there is even an order of knights called the Chevaliers de Sabre d'Or specially for this job) or just by discreetly popping the cork to avoid startling your guests and the wine! Then take your glasses from the ice bucket and fill them quickly – a sparkling delight.

TABLE
Tricks

If you believe everything you see in adverts and films, every good kitchen needs an ice cube machine. But you only need a good old ice cube tray to prove that you can produce impressive results without one. Simply fill it in layers and freeze! Here, the mould was half filled with orange juice, then frozen briefly, topped up with Campari and frozen through. You can even put in some lolly-pop sticks if you like! Important: strong spirits do not freeze (alcohol is an anti-freezing agent!), so they must be diluted. Now even the ice cubes will liven up your cocktails and put everyone in the party mood!

SNACKS AND FINGER FOOD
WITH ENTERTAINMENT VALUE

EN THE BEST PARTIES EVENTUALLY BEGIN TO FLAG ON DRINKS ALONE – YOU NEED
ME SNACKS AND FINGERFOOD, SURPRISING CREATIONS TO SATISFY THOSE WHO ARE
ST A BIT PECKISH AS WELL AS THOSE WHO ALWAYS HAVE ROOM FOR MORE, AND LITTLE
BBLES TO PROVIDE A TALKING POINT AND SET THE PARTY IN FULL SWING. EASY TO
REPARE BUT PRESENTED TO MAXIMUM EFFECT, THIS IS SIMPLY THE BEST IN PARTY FOOD!

JISINE

MINI CLASSICS

JUST AS
WITH ALL GOOD
THINGS IN LIFE, NOT MANY
PEOPLE ADMIT IT BUT EVERYONE
LOVES THEM! THIS IS ESPECIALLY TRUE OF
FAST-FOOD CLASSICS, FROM PIES TO PASTIES AND FROM
BURGERS TO HOTDOGS OR CHIPS. SUCH CULINARY DELICACIES ARE
USUALLY ONLY FOUND IN DUBIOUS AREAS, SERVED IN HUGE TRUCK-DRIVER
PORTIONS! HOWEVER, WHEN SERVED AS CIVILISED NIBBLES, FREE OF GREASE STAINS,
THESE GUILTY PLEASURES ARE CERTAINLY PARTY MATERIAL – HOW ABOUT A MINI-HAMBUR-
GER IN A LITTLE BREAD ROLL, OR A MINI-HOTDOG ON A STICK? GO ON, TREAT YOURSELF!

MINI HOTDOGS ON STICKS

1

Cut the hotdog sausages lengthways into strips.

2

Lay two half-strips across one another and top with slices of gherkin, fried onions or sauces to taste...

For experts

Preparation
approx. 30 mins.

...lay them out on a baking tray, heat under the grill for a few minutes and serve. Delicious!

...and carefully fold up the sausage strips over the filling. Skewer them with cocktail sticks to hold them together...

TABLE TRICKS

These days no one wants big and extravagant – the car industry has proved just how sexy mini can be! The same goes for food – lots of little nibbles are more tantalising than huge portions. Serve little sausages or burgers in miniature straight from the frying pan and mini chips from a little dish, hand out a few cocktail sticks and everyone can pick and choose what they want, dipping in different sauces as they like. This casual style of eating is such a treat and satisfies even the biggest appetites, as long as the tempting treats don't run out too soon! Experience shows that even when you thought you'd prepared too much, there's nothing left at the end! And your guests are happy and satisfied!

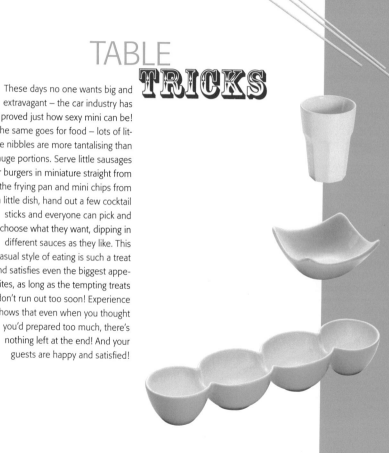

SKEWERED SURPRISES

THE MORE GUESTS YOU HAVE, THE MORE DIFFERENT TASTES YOU'LL HAVE TO CATER FOR. IN ADDITION, THE COMPLICATIONS OF MODERN LIFESTYLES OFTEN MEAN THAT ONE PERSON WON'T EAT FISH, ANOTHER NO MEAT AND THE REST ONLY EAT VEGETABLES. THE HUMBLE SKEWER SOLVES THE DILEMMA AND TURNS THE VARIETY OF TASTES INTO A MYRIAD OF POSSIBILITIES THAT CAN BE PUT ON THE BARBECUE OR PAN-FRIED IN A FLASH. SERVE DIFFERENT DIPPING SAUCES ALONG WITH THEM AND EVEN THE FUSSIEST EATER WILL SOON FIND SOMETHING TO APPEAL TO THEIR TASTEBUDS!

SKEWERED SURPRISE

Even the skewers themselves offer the opportunity to work in a bit of diversity – as well as the traditional kebab skewer, you could use metal or wood skewers...

...or try aromatic alternatives such as lemon grass or sprigs of rosemary...

...thread on chunks of fish, meat, vegetables, herbs or a mixture of all of them...

For 'Skewered surprise' recipe, see pg. 204

...and allow their individual flavours to come out as you grill or fry them. Serve directly from the barbecue, dipped in a variety of sauces – this is party food at its best!

A TASTY BIT ON THE SIDE

...IS WHAT EVERYONE WANTS AT A PARTY. THE SAME GOES FOR THE FOOD – IT TASTES EVEN BETTER WITH A BIT OF BITE! A SOUP CAN BE LIVENED UP WITH A CHOICE OF THINGS TO ADD, FRESH FROM THE GARDEN AND FINELY CHOPPED OR PAN-FRIED TILL THEY'RE CRUNCHY – THE IMPORTANT THING IS TO OFFER THE EYE AND THE TASTE-BUDS A BIT OF VARIETY AND GIVE THE TONGUE SOMETHING TO PLAY WITH – A TASTY BIT ON THE SIDE, YOU MIGHT SAY...

VEGETABLE CRISPS

Peel the potatoes (or even beetroot or radishes) and fry in fresh oil...

Easy
Preparation
approx. 30 mins.

Crisps hardly have a reputation for being luxurious. However, home-made crisps, made from potatoes or other vegetables, are a sensation, and ready in minutes!

...until they're crisp and crunchy. Take them out of the oil and lay them on a thick pile of kitchen paper to soak up the oil, dabbing them if necessary...

Serve the crisps light and airy with a sprinkling of coarsely ground sea salt – perfect!

TABLE TRICKS

Deliciously crunchy and great to look at – these crisps are made of bright purple potatoes (or radishes and beetroot)... the fun is in the variety. Serve the traditional way, wrapped in newspaper like fish and chips, or use greaseproof paper or sandwich paper instead to avoid black marks. Either way, the crisps stay lovely and crunchy!

SWEET TREATS in EGGCUPS

THE SAME GOES FOR DESSERT – LITTLE AND OFTEN BEATS ONE HUGE PORTION. A TWO-TIER PLATTER FULL OF LITTLE DELICACIES OFFERS CHOICE AND VARIETY AND NOT AN OUNCE OF GUILT – NO ONE HAS TO SLAVE AWAY TO EMPTY THE PLATE! WHETHER YOU SERVE TIRAMISU, CRÈME CARAMEL, CHOCOLATE MOUSSE OR JELLY, FRESH FRUIT SORBET OR EVEN ALL OF THEM AT ONCE – THE FUN LIES IN SAMPLING ALL THE DIFFERENT COMBINATIONS! OFF YOU GO!

BERRY SORBET IN EGGCUPS

1

Freeze the berries of your choice (or simply use frozen berries),
leave them to thaw a little then puree with a blender...

...add lemon, or a dash of some delicious
liqueur such as Crème de Cassis or a rich
fruit schnapps to taste...

Fill up the eggcups using an ice cream scoop or two spoons
– yet another sweet temptation!

...either serve the sorbet immediately
or return to the freezer, but before
serving, blend again to give the sorbet
a creamy texture.

TABLE TRICKS

The 'little and often' principle doesn't just apply to food – follow this rule for the table decorations too, and you're on to a winner! Lots of little tea lights provide all the light you need, especially when they're flickering away in eggcups, little dishes or glasses. But be careful – the later you leave them burning, the hotter they will get, so always place them on a bed of salt or sand inside their containers to protect heat-sensitive surfaces. With so many candles, at least one light will carry on burning...

The *art* of sed*ction*

A SPECIAL NIGHT FOR THE MOST IMPORTANT GUEST – LET US SHOW YOU HOW TO CREATE A GOOD FIRST IMPRESSION AND TURN IT INTO A LASTING PASSION... HERE, YOU'LL FIND ENOUGH INSPIRATION TO SET PULSES RACING AND WEDDING BELLS RINGING!

Surprising

treats for the tastebuds

under *the dome*

Kaviar

FLUFFY AND LIGHT MASHED POTATO IS IDEAL FOR HUNDREDS
OF SURPRISES – SERVED IN SMALL PORTIONS AS AN HORS
D'OEUVRE, MASHED POTATO IS CRYING OUT TO BE DRESSED UP
IN SOPHISTICATION – WHY NOT ADD A DASH OF SOUR CREAM
AND CAVIAR; A PERFECT MATCH FOR THE TINGLY SENSATION OF
LUXURIOUS CHAMPAGNE. LET THE EVENING BEGIN!

Mashed potato with truffles

Easy

Preparation approx. 10 mins. + mashed potato preparation

See 'Potato puree' recipe, pg. 207

And when the caviar runs out, it's time to bring out the truffles! Always remember though – the first rule of cookery applies here just as with any other recipe – a chef is only as good as his ingredients. Make sure you buy the best quality products, or even better, use fresh porcini mushroom shavings and enhance the aroma with a splash of truffle oil from a freshly-opened bottle. Either way, it's a fantastic start to a special evening.

TABLE *Tricks*

A crisp, golden slice of toast – the perfect accompaniment to any dish. Be careful though – it doesn't take long for crunchy, piping hot toast to go soft and soggy! The solution: toast stays fresh and crunchy when it's served inside a serviette. Serve with crème fraîche and a spoonful of caviar – you'll be sure to get your reward!

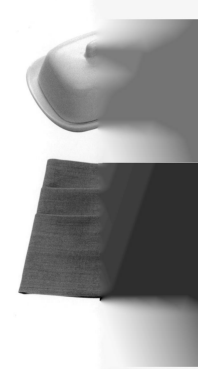

A nest full of health and *vitamins*

A CRISPY SALAD GIVES EVERY MENU A BIT OF BITE, ESPE-
CIALLY WHEN THE SALAD BOWL ITSELF JUST BRINGS YOU
BACK FOR MORE! THIS LITTLE WORK OF ART MADE OF
MELTED PARMESAN LOOKS FABULOUS AND IS SO EASY TO
MAKE – EVEN THE SIMPLEST SALAD HELPS COMPLETE THE
SCENE OF LUXURY. GETTING YOUR VITAMINS HAS NEVER
MADE SUCH A GREAT IMPRESSION.

Crispy Parmesan nests

For 'Colourful leafy salad' recipe, see pg. 208

For experts

Preparation approx. 60 mins. + salad

It really is this simple: grate Parmesan into rough shavings and lay out in circles in a large frying pan or on a baking tray....

...the edges should be a little frayed. Melt
the circles carefully until they turn golden,
keeping a close eye on them...

...then lay each circle over an upturned dish
and press gently into the form of a bowl. As
they cool, the nests will set in shape. Perfect
for presentation, as well as a crispy treat!

ps: a word of warning: if you're planning to
serve a hot soup, a bone china bowl is a safer
choice – these cheese bowls won't stay intact!

TABLE *Tricks*

You don't need to be a Michelin-starred restaurant to arrange your table in style – with extra-large plates and fabric serviettes in napkin rings you can re-create the gourmet restaurant look in your own home. Different glasses for water, white and red wine and different cutlery for each course are the hallmarks of style – and they give a subtle promise of things to come...

Luxury

filet topped

with elegance

THE PIÈCE DE RÉSISTANCE STRAIGHT FROM THE COOKER:
A SUCCULENT FILLET OF FISH OR MEAT, FRIED OR GRILLED,
CAN BE READY IN MINUTES AND PROVIDES ALL THE ENER-
GY YOU NEED FOR THE NIGHT AHEAD...A LIGHT TOPPING
OF VEGETABLE STRIPS ADDS COLOUR AND VITAMINS INTO
THE MIX. THE PERFECT MAIN COURSE, SIMPLE AND READY
IN NO TIME. WELL YOU DON'T WANT TO LEAVE YOUR
GUEST ALONE TOO LONG...

Vegetable ribbon topping

Take some colourful vegetables – the easiest are carrots, Hamburg parsley and courgettes – and, using a peeler or knife, shave them into thin, colourful strips and blanch them briefly...

...when they have cooled, lay the strips together lengthways in colourful bunches...

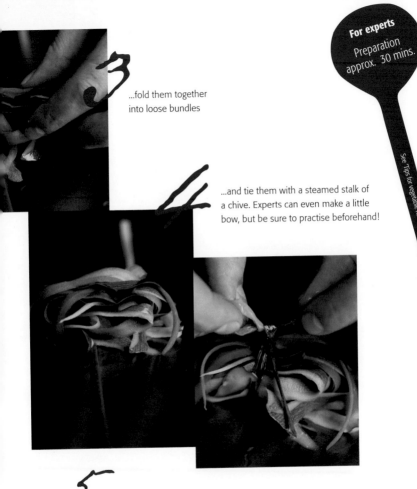

3

...fold them together
into loose bundles

4

...and tie them with a steamed stalk of
a chive. Experts can even make a little
bow, but be sure to practise beforehand!

See Tips for vegetable ribbons on pg. 209

For experts

Preparation
approx. 30 mins.

5

Drizzle the finished vegetable bundles with lemon juice
to prevent discolouring, and put them in the fridge covered so that they stay fresh. Just before serving, cook
and blanch them very briefly in boiling water.

TABLE *Tricks*

Now you know all the tricks of the trade – with a little help from porcelain plates, elegant glasses and classy cutlery even your kitchen table can earn stars of distinction! There are no limits to the fantasy – mood lighting, varied throughout the evening, creates atmosphere, but a few cheerful decorations, such as shells from your last beach holiday together, or a kitsch model Eiffel tower from Paris, don't need words to revive happy memories. If nothing else, why not sprinkle a few kitchen herbs onto the plates, just for good luck!

SOMETHING COOL AND DELICIOUS MAKES
THE PERFECT GRAND FINALE – A SENSUAL
DELIGHT! HERE, THE MELTING SOFTNESS IS
STILL HIDING INSIDE ITS CRUNCHY CONE. IF
YOU HAVE TIME, BAKE THE LITTLE COR-
NETS YOURSELF, IF NOT, THEY ARE READILY
AVAILABLE FROM GOOD DELICATESSENS
AND CONFECTIONERS. THE SAME GOES
FOR THE ICE CREAM – WHETHER IT'S FRESH
FRUIT SORBET OR SOMETHING CREAMY
AND RICH, HOME-MADE OR FROM THE FRO-
ZEN AISLE, IT'S UP TO YOU. IT ALL DEPENDS
ON THE EFFECT YOU WANT TO CREATE.

Crispy treats with a *soft, melting heart*

crispy cornets

For 'Crispy cornets' recipe, see pg. 210

For experts

Preparation approx. 50-60 mins. + filling

Lay out greaseproof paper on a baking tray and draw circles using an upturned bowl...

...then spread out the waffle mixture inside the circles. Important: make sure there are no holes!

They taste fantastic and look even better if you sprinkle finely chopped nuts over the waffle mixture...

Bake briefly according to the recipe and then wrap around a metal mould before you put the cornets into the oven to bake until crisp and golden. Leave to cool!

ps: Well prepared: fill the crispy cornets with your choice of ice cream using a piping bag and put them straight into the freezer so that they don't start to melt before you're ready to serve.

TABLE *Tricks*

When serving these dainty delicacies you need a bit of imagination – you could put coloured sugar in a large dish and place the cornets on top, or be creative with a stemware glass. They're perfect for other decorations too – a sprig of buds or a few flowers will brighten up any table.

A *glass* full of
sweet, sensual
Pleasures

MAKE DESSERT A SIGHT TO BEHOLD – SERVE ON A BE
OF FLOWERS, IN A FLUTE GLASS AND BROUGHT TO
THE TABLE WITH A CRISPY NUT BRITTLE. THIS DESSERT
IS EASILY MADE BUT CREATES A LASTING IMPRESSION.
YOU CAN CHOOSE THE INGREDIENTS TO SUIT YOUR
TASTES – EITHER FRUITY AND LIGHT OR PURE CREAMY
INDULGENCE, THE PRINCIPLE OF THE FLOWER FLUTE
REMAINS THE SAME, AND, LIKE ALL FLOWERS, IT
GUARANTEES TO SEND OUT A SEDUCTIVE AROMA...

Flower flute with crispy nut brittle

For 'Crispy nut brittle' recipe, see pg. 211

Easy

Preparation
approx. 20 mins.
+ dessert

1
Spread thickened fruit sauce (melted chocolate is just as good, dark or white!) around the inside of a flute glass with the back of a spoon...

2
...in the shape of flower petals. Paint them arou the sides of the glass u you have a perfect flow

To make the crispy nut brittle, caramelise some sugar...

...then carefully fill the glass with the dessert of your choice, being careful not to spoil the petal design. And the flower flute is ready to bloom!

...and leave them to cool until you've got the perfect crispy nut brittle!

...pour out in narrow strips...

sprinkle in some chopped nuts
(here we've used colourful pistachios)...

TABLE *Tricks*

Arranged in layers inside a glass, even the simplest ingredients gain instant sophistication. Yoghurt with chocolate sauce? Vanilla cream with strawberry sorbet? Sake mousse with wasabi? Imagination knows no bounds – only your tastes make the rules, but the effect is always impressive. Layered up in a glass, the fillings couldn't look more elegant. And there's still room for decoration on the stem, or choose a fruit to complement the dish and place it in a little dish on top or... whatever you choose, the proof of the pudding is in the eating!

TABLE TRICKS RECIPES

TABLE TRICKS RECIPES

Around the cooking world and back again: from the gels and foams used by 'molecular' chefs to the hearty recipes for more rustic food preferred by the slow food movement; from exploring last blank spots of the culinary world map in the canteen kitchens of deepest Burma to the traditional ingredients of traditional Southern German cookery that crop up in hamburgers. Modern cooking knows no bounds.

Our cooks have chosen the best recipes for this section of Table Tricks, and made them easy and entertaining for everyone: cooking shouldn't be difficult, and everyone around the table should enjoy the end result. There's no need to get too ambitious: a well stocked supermarket or deli will help you cut a few corners. The important thing is that everyone cleans their plate. Remember the saying that empty plates mean good weather the following day. So it's all about making sure that each bite tastes as good as it can...

Sunny start to the day

CLASSIC SCRAMBLED EGGS

1-2 eggs per person
1 tsp butter
salt
pepper

Beat the eggs and then season with salt and pepper. Pour them through a sieve. Next, heat up a non-stick pan and melt the butter in it. Pour in the eggs and let them sit for a moment; then, use a spatula to pull the eggs in from the sides of the pan. The eggs are ready as soon as they have become solid, although they should still be slightly liquid on top.

Easy, great to prepare in advance
Cooking time: 10 mins.
Serves one

TIP 1: for a slightly lighter version, mix in one tablespoon of milk or cream per egg; the taste will be slightly weaker

TIP 2: try serving your eggs with rashers of crispy bacon, thin-cut gammon, or even air-dried ham such as Parma or Serrano

TIP 3: try it with beef jerky, or with cured loin of pork

TIP 4: you could grate some cheese – Emmental, Gouda, Edam, etc. – into the eggs after you've beaten them

TIP 5: mix large chunks of Camembert into the eggs along with Hamburg parsley, cook the eggs, and then serve them with cranberry compôte

TIP 6: you could fry chopped ham, onion and/or bacon in the pan before adding in the eggs

TIP 7: North Sea shrimps, small fried or boiled prawns can either be added in or spread over the eggs

TIP 8: try frying some mushrooms first, pouring the eggs over them and cooking them together (use button mushrooms, shiitake, ceps, oyster mushrooms, chanterelles, morels – anything that tastes good!)

TIP 9: spread strips of smoked salmon or Gravad Lax over the eggs

TIP 10: sprinkle freshly chopped tomatoes over the eggs

TIP 11: fry chopped courgettes, aubergines and peppers over a high heat, add the beaten eggs and cook until done. Sprinkle over sliced olives and chopped tomatoes once ready

TIP 12: fry grated carrots and strips of leek in butter, add in the beaten eggs and cook until done. Then add one slice of fresh goat's cheese and sprinkle with freshly chopped mint and cracked pepper

TIP 13: add cubes of feta cheese, goat's cheese, basil and oregano and then cook carefully, not stirring more than is necessary – serve with fresh tomatoes

MELTED TOMATOES

500g cherry tomatoes
1 tbs olive oil
200 ml passata di tomate (jar or carton of tomato puree)
1 tbs white balsamic vinegar
1 ½ tbs honey or maple syrup
salt, freshly ground black pepper

Slice into the skin of the cherry tomatoes in the shape of a cross and then pour over boiling water; as soon as you have done this, plunge them into cold water and then remove the skins. Bring the oil, tomato puree, balsamic vinegar and honey to a simmer together and then add the tomatoes. Season with salt and pepper.

Easy, great to prepare in advance
Cooking time: 15 mins.
Serves four

TIP 1: go hot with chilli powder or cayenne pepper; add a shot of vodka for a different twist

TIP 2: mix skinned tomatoes with peeled peppers

TIP 3: tear cos lettuce and rocket into small pieces and the pour over the warm melted tomatoes; serve with goat's cheese au gratin (e.g. picandou, crottin de chavignol)

TIP 4: drizzle with excellent olive oil just before serving

page 32

CHOC-NUT MUFFINS

Mixture:
(start with all ingredients at room temperature)
100g butter
80g brown sugar
1 pack of vanilla sugar
zest of half a lemon
pinch of salt
2 large eggs
250g plain white flour
2 tsp baking powder
4-5 tbs full-fat milk
3 tbs roughly-chopped hazelnuts
3 tbs roughly chopped vanilla chocolate

Use a hand mixer to cream the butter with the sugar, vanilla sugar, lemon zest, and salt. Mix in each egg for about 30 seconds, then add in the flour (sifted together with the baking powder) and mix slowly. Add milk as you go along until the mixture is at soft-drop consistency. Portion out the mixture as shown in the photos on page 34/35. Bake at 180°C (fan) or 160°C (without fan) depending on the cup size approx. 15-20 minutes.

Easy, great to prepare in advance
Cooking time: 30-40 mins.
For 6 cups

TIP 1: instead of nuts and chocolate, you could simply add 100g of fresh blueberries or raspberries to the mixture

TIP 2: try adding 3 tbs of dried cranberries and 3 tbs of cubed apple to the mixture

TIP 3: mix in 2 tbs of chopped, dried banana chips and 3 tbs of roasted coconut, smoothing with orange juice

TIP 4: for Christmas – mix in 2 tbs chopped hazelnuts or walnuts, 1 tbs rum soaked raisins, 3 tbs apples, finely chopped, and cinnamon according to taste

page
43

SUGGESTIONS FOR YOUR SANDWICHES

Plain cream cheese, or cream cheese with
herbs, tomatoes, horseradish, or salmon
Cottage cheese
Crème fraîche
Clotted cream
Quark
Vegetarian spread
Guacamole
Apple-horseradish mix
Mayonnaise
Pesto alla genovese
Pesto rosso relishes, chutneys,
and the like

Mustards:
sweet mustard, wholegrain mustard,
Dijon mustard, fig mustard,
honey Dijon mustard

Sweet fillings:
Marmalades, jams, gêlées

TIP: try mixing your cream cheese with freshly chopped herbs such as cress, chives, basil, sorrel, daikon or watercress – keep some of the herb you use in reserve to serve as a garnish. This garnish will help to distinguish various mixtures from one another (see p44/45)

TIP 2: how about tomato cream cheese with freshly chopped tomatoes, or indeed sun-dried tomatoes and basil?

TIP 3: try horseradish with thin cuts of cooked meat, or roast beef with cranberry relish (cranberries can be used to garnish the dish, too – see p 44/45)

TIP 4: smoked salmon and cream cheese with dill mustard

TIP 5: crème fraîche and clotted cream with Gravad Lax, smoked salmon, or even salmon roe, served with lemon

TIP 6: quark with cucumbers, paprika, radishes and salad leaves (cos lettuce hearts, lollo bionda or rosso, lamb's lettuce, endives, baby leaf spinach, spinach)

TIP 7: dijon mustard with scrambled eggs and crispy bacon bits, finely chopped

TIP 8: fig mustard and cheese (Emmental, Gouda, Appenzeller, blue cheeses, goat's cheese, Edam, etc) with slices of apple or pear

TIP 9: exotic relish and chutney with chicken or turkey breast and slices of fresh mango and papaya

TIP 10: try guacamole with fresh cherry tomatoes and strips of carrot

TIP 11: pineapple slices are great with cooked ham on clotted cream or quark

TIP 12: air-dried hams pair very well with pesto and paprika

page 47

MULTI-STOREY SANDWICHES

1.
slices of wholeweat bread, plain cream cheese, smoked salmon, lollo bionda, cream of wasabi, fresh cucumber

2.
white sliced with crispy bacon, turkey breast, slices of tomato, spring onion and garden cress, mayonnaise or aïoli

3.
slices of toast with apple and horseradish, roast beef, lettuce, fried onions; mix wholegrain mustard with some oil and vinegar and dress the topping with it

4.
wholewheat toast with blue cheese, apple and pear slices or quince preserve, lamb's lettuce and chopped, roasted nuts (walnuts or pecan)

5.
thin slices of white tin loaf with plain cream cheese, pesto alla genovese, sun-dried tomatoes in olive oil with rocket and Parma ham

6.
Wholeweat bread, lamb's lettuce, crème fraîche, beetroot, pickled cucumbers, cooked ham, honey Dijon mustard, watercress

7.

toast with guacamole, fried chicken breast cut into strips, slices of mango, mango chutney, avocado and cos lettuce

8.

wholewheat toast with cream cheese and herbs, thin-sliced cucumber, radishes, tomatoes, slices of courgettes, hard-boiled egg, and mayonnaise

9.

wholewheat crispbread with pineapple, freshly-chopped chilli, and thin slices of smoked turkey breast

10.

wholewheat toast with fresh goat's cheese, slices of preserved fig, basil, air-dried ham, dressed with a little honey

11.

very thin slices of wholewheat bread spread with cream cheese, slices of beef à la Bourginonne, wafer thin cooked ham, fresh cabbage salad, cress, and sweet mustard

TIP 1 all forms of toasting bread can be used for these recipes: wheat, three-cereal and wholeweat; tin loaves that you cut yourself, white or brown toast, or even thin, tasty slices of wholewheat bread

TIP 2 you can very well use yesterday's tinned loaf: it will be easier to cut very finely, although you will need to toast it in this case

TIP 3 for a classy edge, you can trim the crusts from the toasting bread

TIP 4 although multi-storey sandwiches may look spectacular, remember that they need to be eaten, too, and you should keep this in mind

TIP 5 you could use cookie cutters to do little designs in the slices of bread

TIP 6 dip the slices of bread into a mixture of beaten egg, milk and perhaps grated Parmesan: you can then fry these wet slices as a form of savoury French toast

TIP 7 or you might like to try writing messages on your bread before toasting it. To do this, you can use a mixture of ½ tsp tomato puree mixed with 1 tbs of hot water and 1 tsp oil; dip a fine brush into this and paint something – a sun, the word love, or the name of the recipient (go for shorter names where possible!)

WHIPPED-UP HERBY SOUP

2 shallots, finely chopped
1 tbs butter
600ml stock (veal, poultry or vegetable)
½ tsp salt
200ml cream
ca. 80-100g mixed fresh herbs
(watercress, sorrel, basil, burnet, borage,
wild garlic, lemon balm)
1 tbs lemon juice
Freshly ground white pepper
2 tbs whipped cream

Sweat the shallots down in the butter and then bring to a low boil with the stock, salt and cream. Cook for 10 minutes. Mix in the freshly chopped herbs with a hand-held mixer. Season to taste with the lemon juice and pepper and, shortly before serving, use the hand-held mixer to whip up the soup before mixing in the cream. Serve immediately.

Easy, great to prepare in advance
Cooking time: 20 mins.
Serves four

TIP! serve this soup with thinly cut garlic bread.

TIP 2: try roasting thin strips of Parma ham (roughly 2cm wide) to a crisp on baking paper in an oven at 200°C. Use kitchen paper to absorb excess fat and serve with the soup and some breadsticks

TIP 3: peel some cucumbers and use a melon baller to cut out small chunks; leave these to cook gently in the warm soup for three to five minutes

CARROT SOUP

500g carrots (diced)
1 onion (diced)
1 tomato (skinned) 750ml chicken stock
Juice of 2 oranges
salt, freshly ground pepper
pinch of cayenne pepper

Cook all ingredients for 25 minutes in a pan with the lid on. Then use either a hand-held mixer or a blender to puree the mixture to a very fine consistency. Season with salt, pepper and cayenne and then pass through a sieve placed over a soup pan. Use a spoon to push any remains through the sieve.

Easy, great to prepare in advance
Cooking time: 20 mins.
Serves four

TIP! try adding a vanilla pod, split open and scraped out, or a walnut-sized piece

of ginger to the mixture as it cooks – finish
the dish with finely chopped Thai basil

TIP 2: mix wild garlic pesto with crème
fraîche; spoon over the soup just before
serving

TIP 3: add in slices of fried beef fillet and
grated horseradish before serving

TIP 1: drizzle some pumpkin seed oil over
the soup and then sprinkle on some roasted
pumpkin seeds

TIP 2: add chopped chillies (hot ones) to the
soup whilst cooking along with the zest and
juice of half a lime. Season with cinnamon

TIP 3: try coconut milk as an alternative to
cream

page
53

PUMPKIN SOUP

**500g diced pumpkin flesh
(e.g. Hokkaido squash, nutmeg pumpkin)
1 onion (diced)
1 clove of garlic (chopped)
400 ml vegetable stock
200 ml cream
Salt, freshly ground pepper
3 tbs fresh orange juice**

Cook all the ingredients together at medium temperature for 25 minutes. The use a hand-held
mixer or a blender to puree the soup to a very
fine consistency. Season with salt, pepper, and
orange juice.

Easy, great to prepare in advance
Cooking time: 35 mins.
Serves four

page
54

PRAWNS ON A PASTA NEST

**2 tsb turmeric
500g spaghetti
2 tsb butter
1 small packet of saffron
600g black tiger prawns (peeled)
2 tsb olive oil
1 garlic clove (chopped)
2 red Thai chillies cut into thin slices
½ tsp sea salt
Freshly cracked pepper
½ bunch of Hamburg parsley,
roughly chopped**

Add the turmeric to 5l of boiling water and then
cook the spaghetti al dente in this water. Melt the
butter and stir in the saffron. Fry the prawns in hot
olive oil and then turn down the heat. Add the

garlic, Thai chillies and seasoning, and cook for as long as the size of the prawns requires. Finish by stirring in the parsley. Coat the cooked spaghetti in the saffron butter and serve as shown in the photo feature on pages 56 and 57. Place the prawns on top of this.

Easy, great to prepare in advance
Cooking time: 20 mins.

Serves four

TIP!

TIP 1: coat basil, rosemary and oregano in hot oil and use as a garnish instead of parsley

TIP 2: towards the end of the cooking time, add some long, thin slices of carrot and leek to the spaghetti and serve everything with grated Pecorino, Manchego or Parmesan cheese as vegetable spaghetti

TIP 3: serve the spaghetti with crisply fried lamb fillet, seasoned with lemon thyme, garlic and lime juice. Slice the fillets thinly and arrange on the spaghetti

page 58

SPRINGTIME PASTA

TOMATO SAUCE

2 tbs olive oil
1 onion (chopped)
1 clove garlic (chopped)
1 t tbs tomato purée
600g ripe tomatoes
125 ml vegetable, chicken or veal stock
salt, pepper, sugar

Sweat the onion and garlic in the hot olive oil, stir in the tomato purée and fry until slightly browned. Cut the tomatoes into big chunks, add to the onion-garlic mixture, and then deglaze the pan with the stock. Cook at a slow boil, covered, for 10 minutes. Use a hand-held mixer to puree the sauce to a very fine consistency and then pass through a sieve. Throw away the tomato skins and seeds. Allow the sauce to cook down to a thicker consistency and then season with salt, pepper and sugar.

Easy, great to prepare in advance
Cooking time: 25 mins.

Serves four

TIP!

TIP 1: add chopped basil, freshly diced tomato and chopped pine nuts just before serving

CHEESE SAUCE

1 shallot (chopped)
1 tsp butter
200 ml cream
125 ml stock (vegetable, poultry, or veal)
150 g cream, cream cheese
salt, pepper, nutmeg
80 g Parmesan (finely grated)

Sweat down the shallots in hot butter, pour in the cream and stock, and bring to the boil. Turn down the heat and stir in the cream cheese, melting it slowly. Finally, add in the Parmesan and allow it to melt into the sauce.

Easy, great to prepare in advance
Cooking time: 15 mins.
Serves four

TIP!

TIP! try adding freshly grated lemon zest and a squirt of lemon juice.

HERB SAUCE

1 ½ tbs butter
1 ½ level tbs flour
125ml cream
125 ml full fat milk
150 ml vegetable stock
salt, nutmeg
5 tbs chopped herbs e.g. parsley, chervil, chives, tarragon

Melt the butter in the pan and stir in the flour. Pour in the cream and milk (cold), stir vigorously to blend and bring to the boil for a short while. Add in the stock and taste for seasoning. Mix in the herbs just before serving.

Easy, great to prepare in advance
Cooking time: 20 mins.
Serves four

TIP! mix 2 egg yolks into the warm sauce – do not bring to the boil after this step

page 61

STUFFED LUMACHE

250 g lumache pasta ("snails")
2 tbs olive oil
200 g Shiitake mushrooms (cut into slices)
1 courgette (finely diced)
1 red pepper (diced)
100 g green olives (cut into slices)
3 tbs Pesto alla genovese
200 ml vegetable stock
1 tbs lemon juice
1 level tbs starch
1 egg yolk
2 tbs cold butter
some Hamburg parsley, some sage leaves
3 tbs freshly-grated Parmesan (or other cheese) for baking the pasta

Cook the pasta in boiling, salted water until it is al dente. Fry the mushrooms in hot olive oil, then add the courgette and paprika whilst stirring, cooking for a further 3-5 minutes. Then mix in the pesto and olives. Stuff this mixture into the cooked lumache with a teaspoon. Spread the pasta forms out on plates, and bring the stock - with the lemon juice – to the boil. Continue by whisking the starch into water to get a smooth mixture and then adding this to the stock. Take the sauce off the stove and add in the egg yolk and butter. Pour the sauce over the pasta, sprinkle the cheese over this, and bake briefly in the oven.

Medium, great to prepare in advance
Cooking time: 30 mins.
Serves four

TIP!

TIP : just before serving, drizzle a little truffle oil over the pasta and take it to the table as quickly as possible

page 62

CELERIAC PUREE

600g celeriac, peeled and roughly diced
100g cold butter
4 tbs full fat milk
salt, freshly-ground pepper
grated nutmeg

Cook the celeriac in boiling water until very tender. Drain and then combine with the butter and milk using a hand-held blender or mixer. Season to taste.

Easy, great to prepare in advance
Cooking time: 20 mins.
Serves four to six

PARSNIP MASH

400g parsnips, peeled and roughly
chopped
2 floury potatoes, peeled and cut into
large chunks
1 small clove garlic, chopped
100g cold butter
80ml full fat milk
salt, freshly-ground pepper

Cook the parsnips, potatoes and garlic in salted water until very tender. Drain and use a hand-held blender or mixer to combine with the butter and milk. Season to taste.

Easy, great to prepare in advance
Cooking time: 20 mins.
Serves fout to six

MASHED SWEDE

1 small swede, approx. 800g
100g butter
125ml chicken or vegetable stock
salt, freshly ground pepper
pinch of cinnamon and cayenne pepper

Cut away the outer skin on the swede and then cut swede into big chunks. Boil until very tender, drain, and use a hand-held blender or mixer to combine with the butter and stock. Season to taste.

Easy, great to prepare in advance
Cooking time: 20 mins.
Serves four to six

TIP 1: you can mix the various mashes and purees together or with mashed potatoes according to your taste (see p. 207 for mashed potatoes) in order to make their flavour less intensive

TIP 2: try mixing in/sprinkling over chopped herbs such as parsley, chives, lovage, watercress, wild garlic, sorrel, etc.

TIP 3: you could also think about adding other ingredients to change the flavour or texture of your purees and mash. Some suggestions:
- chopped, roasted nuts (almonds, pine nuts, walnuts)
- fried cubes of pancetta (or milder Italian speck), or of another variety of smoked bacon
- grilled strips of air-dried ham (Serrano, Parma)
- grated cheese, e.g. Parmesan, Pecorino, Appenzeller etc.
- Strips of sun-dried tomatoes preserved in oil.

RECIPE PLUS
"BEETROOT, RADISH AND POTATO PUREE TOWERS"

Instead of radish and beetroot, you could try the following. Whichever ingredients you use, though, slice them thinly!

TIP 1: courgette and aubergine
TIP 2: turnip and big slices of carrot

TIP 3: kohlrabi and beetroot

TIP 4: parsnip and apple – with blue potato mash – with fried calf's liver and pan juices: simply delicious! (Prepare the apple carefully: it can fall apart in the blanching and cutting stages)

TIP 5: Jerusalem artichokes and turnips

WITH SEARED MEAT

TIP 1: the best kind of pan to use for meat is a non-stick pan, or even a cast-iron pan if you have one

TIP 2: you should always warm the pan through without fat before adding oil or butter – the fat will then come to temperature more quickly and you can start cooking the meat straightaway

TIP 3: as always, less is more. Two pieces of beef only need ½ tsp oil for frying. An even better method is to oil the meat rather than the pan, and to only add butter at the last moment

TIP 4: never put a lid on the pan whilst searing meat: you will essentially create a "steamer" and the meat will boil rather than fry

TIP 5: Some people are convinced that you should season meat before frying. Others say afterwards. Which is correct? The answer is: both! It simply depends on your taste

TIP 6: you should leave seared meat to rest wrapped in aluminium foil (coated side to

the meat so as to reflect heat back at the meat and finish the cooking process)

TIP 7: remember to take the cut of meat you want to fry out of the fridge well before you intend to start cooking: it should always be at room temperature to begin with to stop it bleeding too much

TIP 8: this is also the case for frozen meat: be sure to let it thaw thoroughly beforehand

TIP 9: Before frying, dry the meat as much as possible with kitchen roll

TIP 10: whilst frying, be careful when turning the meat. Only use a blunt tool – never a fork, which might pierce the meat, leading to it losing its juices and becoming dry

TIP 11: the cooking time depends on the weight and thickness of the meat, as well as the level of cooking you want. By using your finger to press lightly on the meat during cooking, you can see how well done it is. As a general rule: the more malleable the meat, the less cooked it is. Conversely, the harder it is, the closer it is to being cooked through.

Furthermore, if juices escape from the meat, you can tell by the colour how far along the meat is. The redder the juices, the less cooked the meat. Clearer juices, however, mean that the meat is more done

TIP 12: if you want to cook a fillet steak weighing 200g to medium doneness, it should be seared for 2 minutes 30 seconds and left to rest for 3 minutes in aluminium foil in a warm oven

COOKING WITH Friends

TIP!

ALL ABOUT SASHIMI

TIP 1: When you're making sashimi at home, the more solid types of fish such as tuna, salmon, turbot, cod and mackerel are better. Be sure to ask your fishmonger for his recommendation: the fresher the better

TIP 2: Have the fishmonger cut the fish evenly and as thin as possible

TIP 3: Get the fish wrapped as tightly as possible in cling-film and keep very cold (use an insulated bag if your journey home is a long one!)

TIP 4: : Try different cuts of the same fish (especially with tuna).

Easy / Preparation time: 5 mins.

SESAME TWISTS

1 egg white
3-4 tbs flour
1 ½ tbs lime juice
½ tsp salt
1-2 tbs oil or melted butter
150g black sesame
baking parchment
oil to grease the wooden spoon

Mix the ingredients together to form a smooth, slightly fluid batter. If the egg white is on the small side, you might want to add more lime juice. Leave the batter to rest for 30 minutes, covered. Beat the batter again and then put into a piping bag with a very small hole. If you don't have a piping bag, you can use a teaspoon to spread the batter over the sesame seeds. Work with the batter as shown on page 74/75 (step 1). With the oven at either 160°C with fan or 180°C without, bake for two minutes. Then proceed as outlined in step 2. With the oven at the same temperature, bake the twists again for 12-15 minutes until golden brown (timing depends on the speed of your oven). Once baked, carefully remove the sesame twists from the paper – be careful, they are fragile! You'll need to develop a feeling for it, so be prepared to break a few at the start...

For experts, great to prepare in advance
Cooking time: 45 mins.

TIP!

TIP 1: make sure the wooden spoon you are using is well greased so that the twists do not stick

TIP 2: start by baking smaller twists. Once you've got the hang of it, you can try your hand at longer ones

TIP 3: try working some sesame oil into the batter for an extra nutty flavour

SHARI (SOUR RICE)

2 cups of sushi rice
4 tsb rice vinegar
2 tbs sugar
1 tsp salt

First, wash the rice under running water until the water runs clear. Put the rice into a saucepan with at least 2 cups of water. Wrap a lid in a kitchen towel and press down hard onto the pan: this will prevent steam escaping. Bring the rice to the boil, turn down the heat, and steam for 15 minutes. Next, remove the pan from the hob, place a dry kitchen towel around the lid and leave it to stand for 15 minutes. Using a wooden spoon, mix 4 tbs rice vinegar with 2 tbs sugar and 1 tsp salt in a porcelain bowl placed over steam water. Put the rice into a bowl while it is still warm, pour over the mixture, and use the wooden spoon to mix the two together. As you are doing this, use a fan or some cardboard to cool down the rice.

Easy, great to prepare in advance
Cooking time: 35 mins.
Serves two to four

Serving suggestions: :
TIP 1: paper-thin slices of cucumber, plain or marinated in chilli sauce
TIP 2: paper-thin slices of fresh daikon radish
TIP 3: paper-thin slices of preserved yellow radish (takuan)

TIP 4: carrots cut lengthways into paper-thin strips (you might even need to do this with a peeler!)
TIP 5: fried shiitake mushrooms
TIP 6: amazu shoga (ginger preserved in a sweet and sour sauce, can be purchased)
TIP 7: daikon leaves
TIP 8: sesame seed for sprinkling – you might want to roast them in a dry non-stick pan or with a little oil in order to strengthen the nutty flavour
TIP 9: salmon roe
TIP 10: japanese soy or shoyu sauce: light (usu-kuchi) or dark (koi-kuchi), the latter is a rather light, flavoursome sauce. Chinese soy sauce tends to be saltier, smokier, and not a traditional partner for sashimi and the like
TIP 11: tamari or soy sauce – preferably organic
TIP 12: wasabi hot horseradish paste from a tube or made up from powder
TIP 13: try serving a glass noodle salad with seaweed and vegetables as a side dish. Cover the noodles in boiling water, leave them to swell, drain them, and then mix with soy, lime juice and zest, some sugar or maple syrup, finely-chopped spring onion and nori (sea-weed for sushi), as well as finely chopped chillies. Finish the dish with finely chopped blanched mange-touts

page 78

ZIG ZAG ZUCCHINI

FILLING Nº.1

2 tbs diced bacon
1 shallot, chopped
1 tsp butter
200g red cabbage (cut into strips)
1 apple, peeled, finely diced
3 tbs balsamic vinegar
1 tsp honey
1 tbs plum jam
2 tbs soy sauce
100g chanterelle mushrooms, cleaned

Fry the diced bacon and onion. Mix in the butter, red cabbage and apple together and fry for three minutes whilst stirring. Deglaze with the balsamic vinegar, add honey, the plum jam and soy sauce, along with the mushrooms and cook for a further two minutes. Prepare the courgettes as shown on p. 80/81 and divide the mixture between the four portions. Grease a big baking dish and place the stuffed courgettes in it.

Medium, great to prepare in advance
Cooking time: 45 mins.
Serves four

FILLING Nº.2

200g mushrooms
1 onion, chopped
2 tbs butter
1 pear, finely diced
100g cherry tomatoes, cut into four
salt, pepper

Cut the mushrooms into small pieces and sweat them down with the onions in hot butter. Add the pear and tomato and cook for a further three minutes or so. Season the mixture and use it to stuff the remaining four courgettes. Place them into a baking dish, pour over 125ml chicken stock and cook at 160°C (fan) or 180°C (without fan) for 15-20 minutes.

Easy, great to prepare in advance
Cooking time: 30 mins.
Serves four

TIP 1: small aubergines, pre-cooked and hollowed out, are just as good for stuffing as courgettes, along with the following vegetables
TIP 2: small peppers (all colours)
TIP 3: pre-cooked kohlrabi
TIP 4: pre-cooked beetroot
TIP 5: tomatoes that are not too ripe
TIP 6: pre-cooked turnips
TIP 7: big, stuffed mushrooms are always a big hit
TIP 8: try small pumpkins (mini-patissons, small Hokkaidos, rounded moschus squash)

TIP 11: you can vary the stuffing – e.g. rata-touille, feta cheese

TIP 10: try using pre-cooked onions

TIP 11: mincemeat and sauerkraut make an excellent combination, as well as

TIP 12: vegetable couscous

TIP 13: : various risottos

TIP 14: fish stuffing – not just for Fridays, you know!

TIP 14: stews with chicken, game, rabbit or fish make great alternatives

page
84

SEA BREAM PARCEL

1 sheet of baking parchment
1-2 tbs oil (olive oil for a Mediterranean or exotic recipe, plain oil for a northern European version)
1 sea bream (silver or red), approx. 800g, prepared
salt, freshly ground pepper
1 lime/lemon
3 cloves of garlic, in their skins, slightly crushed
2 shallots
1 tbs butter
2 tbs white wine
herbs according to your taste
– Mediterranean, Asian, or Nordic –
see the following

MEDITERRANEAN BREAM

2 sprigs of oregano
2 branches of rosemary
3 branches of thyme
2 sprigs of basil
2-3 bay leaves

ASIA STYLE BREAM

2 stalks of lemongrass, cut into small pieces, slightly bruised
4 stalks of coriander
2 garlic chives
4 kaffir lime leaves

NORDIC BREAM

4 sprigs parsley
2 sprigs dill
handful chives
2 bay leaves
1-2 sprigs lovage

Grease the baking parchment with the oil. Wash the bream and season with salt and pepper inside and out. Place on the parchment, cut a lime or lemon into slices and fill the inside with them. Slice the garlic and shallots and place them next to the citrus slices. Season with herbs both inside and outside as you like, dot with butter and drizzle white wine over the fish. Use the parchment and butcher's twine to tie up the fish into a package.

Bake for 20-40 minutes in the oven (180°C fan, 200°C without).

Easy, great to prepare in advance
Cooking time: 40-60 mins.
Serves two

APPLE TART

4 sheets frozen millefeuille pastry
1 tbs butter
4 apples, with stalks,
e.g. Elstar, Cox Orange
Juice ½ lemon
1 egg yolk
2 tbs Calvados

Allow the pastry to thaw and roll it out to the same size as the dish you intend to use. Firstly, fold it back on itself and roll it out to the size you require at about ¾ cm. Lay it in a buttered dish, peel and halve the apple, core it, but leave the stalk. Sprinkle with lemon juice, and then cut the apple as shown on pages 92/93. Spread the apple slices out of the pastry and brush over the egg-yolk/Calvados mixture; bake for approx. 10-15 minutes at 180°C (fan) or 200°C (without).

Easy, great to prepare in advance
Cooking time: 30-40 mins.
Serves four

TIP 1: try serving with vanilla sauce, vanilla quark, cinnamon cream, cranberry cream or chocolate sauce

TIP 2: instead of millefeuille, you could try using filo pastry. If you use it, cut it into a rectangular shape, slightly bigger than the form you are using. You should baste each single sheet with butter and sugar; lay 6 to 8 sheets over each other. Apart from that, the recipe remains unchanged

TIP 3: you can also use short-crust pastry in this recipe. Knead together 80g sugar, 160g butter, 240g flour and then put the dough in the fridge. Divide the pastry into four portions, roll it out to fit the dishes, put it in the buttered dishes, and continue as in the recipe

Happy Hour

page
106

FRESH AND FRUITY

RASPBERRY SMOOTHIE

200g raspberries
200ml cherry juice
4 tbs raspberry syrup
200g cream yoghurt

Combine everything in a mixer and serve in glasses.

Easy, great to prepare in advance
Preparation time: 5-10 mins.
Serves two to four

TIP 1: try replacing the cream with sparkling wine or Prosecco and a shot of Campari. Serve ice-cold.

BANANA FLIP

2 ripe bananas
6 scoops vanilla ice cream
300ml milk

Puree everything in a blender and serve in glasses.

Easy / Preparation time: 5-10 mins.
Serves four

TIP 1: Serve in glasses that have been in the freezer with cream on top, chocolate sprinkles and some advocaat

CHOCO SHAKE

4 scoops vanilla ice cream
2 scoops chocolate ice cream
250ml coco
200ml coconut milk

Blend everything together in a mixer. Put 2-3 ice-cubes into mugs and then pour in the shake.

Easy / Preparation time: 5-10 mins.
Serves two to four

TIP 1: try drizzling each serving with 1-2 tbs coffee liqueur

page
112

BELLINI

2 ripe peaches
450 ml Prosecco

Extract the juice from the peaches. Smooth with 2 tbs Prosecco and pour in glasses. Fill in the Prosecco as shown on p. 80/81.

Easy / Preparation time: 30 mins.
Serves four

TIP 1: if there's no juicer at hand: plunge peaches into boiling water, remove immediately and then plunge into cold water. Skin should slip off easily. Press through a sieve to puree
TIP 2: try using liqueur according to taste instead of Prosecco to smooth
TIP 3: it works with every sparkling wine – but with Prosecco it won't foam as much as others

page
119

CAMPARI-ORANGE
ICE CUBES

200 ml orange juice, chilled
50 ml Campari
100 ml water
16 sticks

Mix the water with the Campari – otherwise it won't freeze and fill in ice-cube tray. Freeze slightly in the freezer approx. 15 mins. Carefully put the sticks in and fill up with the ice-cold orange juice. Freeze overnight.

Easy, great to prepare in advance
Preparation time: 30 mins. plus freezing time
For approx. 14 ice cubes

TIP 1: instead of Campari use Pimms No.1 – just be sure to water down the alcohol so it will freeze

page 124

MINI HOTDOGS ON A STICK

4 mini hotdogs
4 gherkins (sliced)
4 tbs fried onions
4 tbs honey-mustard dressing
4 thin slices white bread
2 tb curry powder
16 cocktail sticks

Cut the sausages lengthways into 4 slices, and cut these slices in half. Lay two slices across each other and then place some gherkin, onions, and mustard in the middle. Fold the sausages over one another, and fasten them to the bread with cocktail sticks. Put them on baking parchment in a roasting tin and then put them at the bottom of the oven (160°C with fan, 180°C without). Bake for 8-10 minutes until crisp. Serve with a dusting of curry powder.

For experts, great to prepare in advance
Cooking time: 30 mins.
For 16 mini hotdogs

TIP 1: if you just can't enjoy your hotdog without a good dollop of typical salad cream, just bring it to the table as a dip

HOMEMADE CURRY SAUCE

1 tbs coriander seeds
1 tbs olive oil
4 tomatoes, skinned and finely chopped
1 piece of ginger (about the size of the end of your finger, chopped finely)
200ml tomato passata (bottle or tetrapak)
2 tbs apple vinegar
4 tbs neutral, clear honey
sea salt
curry seasoning of your choice

Start by dry-frying the coriander seeds in a pan and then crushing them with a pestle and mortar. Fry the tomato and ginger in hot olive oil and add the passata. Mix in the vinegar and the honey and then leave to simmer with a lid of for 5 minutes. Use a hand-held mixer to puree the mixture, reduce it somewhat, add salt, and then season with the coriander and curry powder.

Easy, great to prepare in advance
Cooking time: 20 mins.

TIP 1: try using apricot jam instead of honey

SALMON CHILLI MINT KEBAB

approx. 250g thick-cut salmon fillet
cut into 12 pieces
½ lime cut into slices
4 red Thai chillies
2 sprigs mint
4 stalks lemon grass

TUNA AND PEPPER CHILLI KEBAB

approx. 250g tuna fillet
cut into 12 pieces
½ red pepper cut into short, fat strips
about 1cm thick
2 sprigs coriander
4 Thai chillies
4 stalks lemon grass

SALMON-LEMON-TOMATO KEBAB

approx. 250g salmon fillet
cut into 12 pieces
½ lemon cut into slices
6 cherry tomatoes, halved
4 small rosemary sprigs

MARINADE

2 tbs lime juice
2 tbs light soy sauce
2 tsp maple syrup
1 tsp sesame oil
1 tsp olive oil

Take the ingredients and place them alternately on the stalks of lemon grass or rosemary. For the marinade, mix the ingredients together and spread over the kebabs before and after cooking – you might want to scatter over some sesame seeds as well. Grill or fry the kebabs for two minutes on each side.

Easy, great to prepare in advance
Preparation time: 30 mins.
Serves four

TIP!

TIP 1: You can "pre-drill" the fish fillet with a wooden kebab stick so that it slips onto the rosemary branch more easily

DIPS FOR YOUR STICKS

TIP 1: Asian sweet and sour dip
TIP 2: Asian hot and spicy dip
TIP 3: soy sauce with sesame seeds
TIP 4: hoi-sin sauce
TIP 5: crèma di balsamico
TIP 6: picada (Catalan garlic dip)

TIP 7: pesto alla genovese
TIP 8: wild garlic pesto
TIP 9: pesto rosso
TIP 10: guacamole
TIP 11: aioli
TIP 12: rouille
TIP 13: wasabi-crème fraîche
TIP 14: mint yoghurt with cracked pepper
TIP 15: chutneys and pickles, e.g.: mango,
pepper, pumpkin
TIP 16: barbecue sauce

SAUCES FOR YOUR STICKS

TIP 1: peanut butter sauce
TIP 2: chilli and garlic sauce
TIP 3: lemon or lime butter
TIP 4: coconut and coriander sauce
TIP 5: hot and spicy tomato sauce
TIP 6: curry sauce
TIP 7: salsa Mallorquina
TIP 8: salsa verde
TIP 9: green sauce
TIP 10: horseradish sauce
TIP 11: red wine and shallot butter
TIP 12: pepper sauce
TIP 13: hot cress sauce

page
184

TWO KINDS OF DIP FOR VEGETABLE CHIPS

SOUR CREAM CHEESE DIP

200g sour or clotted cream
150g soft cheese
100g blue cheese
1 spring onion
2 wild garlic leaves
sea salt, pepper

Mix the cream (sour or clotted), cheeses (soft and blue) together until smooth and creamy. Season with sea salt and cracked pepper. Chop the spring onion and wild garlic and mix into the dip.

Easy, great to prepare in advance
Preparation time: 15 mins.

TIP 1: Try mixing in 2 tbs tinned cranberries
TIP 2: Or try adding 4 tbs stewed pears
TIP 3: You could use fresh goat's cheese, adding chopped, roasted pecans and mint leaves cut into strips

AVOCADO AND TOMATO DIP

2 big, ripe avocados
juice of 1½ oranges
juice of ½ lemon
3 tomatoes
2 sprigs coriander
sea salt, pepper

Work the avocados into a fine puree with the orange and lemon juice. Skin the tomatoes, chop them into four, remove the seeds and dice finely. Season with salt and pepper, mix in the chopped tomatoes, and add the chopped coriander leaves.

Easy / Preparation time: 15 mins.

TIP 1: you could mix in 2 tbs diced yellow pepper, 1 chopped clove garlic and 2 tbs chopped cucumber

TIP 2: 2 tbs diced mango and ½ chopped chilli make a good addition

TIP 3: mix in some chopped basil, parsley and chives

TIPS FOR DEEP FRYING

TIP 1: not all oils are suitable for high temperatures. Peanut oil is the best for heating, and some mixtures are also good – which are available in health food stores. Olive oil heats well, but many find it too strong. It can also turn bitter if used to fry

TIP 2: using coconut oil or similar products for deep frying is completely old fashioned – doing so is incredibly unhealthy

TIP 3: take a pan with high sides, or a saucepan, and fill it with oil 2 cm high. Heat it through on a medium hob for 3 to 5 minutes

TIP 4: you can use a wooden kebab stick to measure the heat: simply hold it in the oil. If little bubbles gather around is, the oil is hot enough for you to start deep frying!

TIP 5: an even better way to deep fry is to use a deep fat fryer; you'll be able to set and keep the oil temperature steady. They are a devil to clean, though!

TIP 6: do not fry at over 175°C – at this point, carcinogenic acrylamides start to form

TIP 7: do not try to fry too much at once; each piece of food should be able to "swim freely"

TIP 8: you should not use the same oil more than two or three times

TIP 9: always leave your deep-fried food to dry on kitchen paper in order to remove excess grease

Dinner à Deux

STRAWBERRY SORBET

**1 packet of frozen strawberries, approx.
350g
50g icing sugar
Juice 1 lemon
150ml strawberry syrup
1-2 tbs Crème de Cassis**

Put the strawberries into a high-sided container and leave them to thaw slightly and then, using a hand-held blender, puree them batch by batch into the other ingredients. Divide into portions and serve immediately.

Easy, great to prepare in advance
Preparation time: 30 mins.
Serves four

TIP 1: try replacing the syrup with sparkling wine, Champagne or Prosecco
TIP 2: if you mix in a fresh egg white, your sorbet will become creamier
TIP 3: this recipe works just as well with raspberries, blueberries, cherries, apricots, redcurrants, blackberries or a mix of several
TIP 4: instead of syrup, try using yoghurt, milk, cream or buttermilk

MASHED POTATO

**750g floury potatoes, peeled
100ml milk
100g butter
salt, pepper, nutmeg**

Cut the potatoes into large chunks and cook in boiling salted water with a lid on the pan. Drain them and let them steam for a while on the stove; pass the cooked potatoes through a potato press or mash them by hand. Warm the milk and butter and then use a whisk to blend the dairy products into the potatoes. Keep whisking until the puree is creamy. Season with salt, pepper, and nutmeg, perhaps mixing in more butter if required, or desired!

Easy, great to prepare in advance
Cooking time: 30 mins.
Serves four to six

TOPPINGS

TIP 1: sour cream and caviar
TIP 2: freshly grated truffle or fried ceps, along with truffle oil
TIP 3: freshly grated Parmesan and Crema di balsamico

TIP 4: herbs, briefly deep fried: Hamburg parsley, chervil, or sage
TIP 5: clotted cream, shrimp and dill
TIP 6: watercress with a light Dijon mustard dressing
TIP 7: tartar of fresh Gravad Lax or smoked salmon, prepared with wasabi and sprouts
TIP 8: croûtons and crispy diced speck
TIP9: cooked asparagus, chopped, with Hamburg parsley cut into strips and butter

EXCITING LEAF SALADS

200g mixed leaf salad:
e.g.: baby leaves or lamb's lettuce with frisée, radicchio; or cos and rocket or oakleaf, with lollo bionda and lamb's lettuce; or endives and mixed leaves; there are many variations as there are people

BASIC DRESSING

1 shallot, finely chopped
3-4 tbs balsamic vinegar
3 tbs water
1 tsp honey mustard
½ tsp sugar
½ tsp salt
6 tsb olive oil (extra virgin), or rape seed oil or sunflower seed oil for a more neutral flavour

Wash the salad thoroughly, leave to drip dry and, if you have one, use a lettuce drier to spin the leaves dry. Tear the salad into bite-sized pieces and place in a bowl. For the dressing: mix all the ingredients except the oil, leave to stand, and then beat in the oil. Pour over the salad and serve.

Easy, great to prepare in advance
Preparation time: 15 mins.
Serves four

TIP 1: sprinkle with roasted walnut and pine nuts
TIP 2: sprinkle roasted sesame seeds over the salad
TIP 3: try adding fresh berries: e.g. raspberries and blueberries
TIP 4: place some croûtons on the salad
TIP 5: you can break crispy bacon into bits and sprinkle these over the salad
TIP 6: try adding sliced olives and/or capers

page
162

VEGETABLE GARNISH

This garnish is suitable for/on top of the following:

Breast of guinea fowl
Venison medallion
Lamb fillet
Salmon fillet
Sea bass fillet
Tuna fillet
Turbot
Beef fillet
Pork fillet
Roast beef
Chicken breast
Turkey breast
Rump of pork ...

All of these can be fried, grilled, roasted/baked or, of course, steamed.

TIPS ON FRYING FISH

TIP 1: the best kind of pan to use for fish is a non-stick pan, or even a cast-iron pan if you have one

TIP 2: You should always warm the pan through without fat before adding oil or butter – the fat will then come to temperature more quickly and you can start cooking the fish straightaway

TIP 3: use kitchen paper to dry the fish as thoroughly as possible before frying

TIP 4: turn the fish in flour and dust off excess, leaving a thin layer on the fish. This will stop the fish sticking in to pan (especially plaice, sole, etc). It will also give you a lovely brown crust.

TIP 5: as opposed to meat, fish needs a lot of fat in the pan – e.g. two pike fillets at 200g will require 1 ½ tbs oil, butter or melted butter

TIP 6: Use a flavourless oil to fry fish, e.g. rape seed oil, peanut oil; for a Mediterranean flavour, or if you just like it, use olive oil

TIP 7: try flavouring the oil before frying: e.g. heat it lightly and add garlic, lemon or lime zest, rosemary, thyme, etc. Fry these ingredients gently and then remove them before frying the fish.

TIP 8: fish takes far less time to cook than meat, and is usually served just cooked. You should fry each side at a high heat for about 1 minute before turning down the heat, turning the fish, and finishing the cooking according to thickness and weight. As a guide, a pike fillets at 200g will take 2-5 minutes to cook.

TIP 9: Exception: salmon and red tuna fillets (roughly 2cm thick) done "new Asian style". Here, you should fry the fish very quickly at a high temperature in order to create a crust. The fish should remain raw on the inside, however. Serve with soy sauce, fresh herbs, freshly cracked peppercorns, chopped ginger and, if you like the idea, lime juice and maple syrup, with a little lime zest. Simply delicious!

TIP 10: if you have a whole fish to fry (e.g. red mullet, smaller sea bass), fry it briefly first and then put it in the oven (200°C without fan or 180°C with) and finish for 8-10 minutes

TIP 11: you can season the fish either before or after cooking

TIP 12: if you've got an entire fish, fill the central cavity with herbs

CRISPY CORNETS

180g sugar
60g Marzipan
3 eggs
zest of ½ 1 unwaxed orange
pinch of salt
150g plain flour
1-2 tsp cream
2 tbs sesame seeds

For the baking tray:
baking parchment
1 tbs melted unsalted butter or neutral cooking oil e.g. peanut oil
1 tbs plain flour

Take the marzipan and cube it. Press it together with the orange, salt and 1 egg and mix with a fork. Using an electric whisk, beat the remaining two eggs thoroughly into the mixture until it is smooth. Sieve the flour and work into the mixture with a whisk before leaving the mixture to rest, covered, for about 30 minutes. Lightly grease the baking paper and dust with flour. Mix in the cream and then place the dough on the baking tray as shown on p 170/171. In order to bake all cornetti to an even, golden crisp, you'll need to pre-bake them for 4-5 minutes at 180°C (without fan) or 160°C (fan-assisted). Allow to cool and then bake for another 4-5 minutes until golden brown.

For experts, great to prepare in advance
Cooking time: 50-60 mins.
Serves four

TIP 1: Instead of sesame seeds, you could try sprinkling chopped almonds or hazelnuts on the mixture

TIP 2: Instead of cream, you can use beetroot juice or red food colouring to turn your cornets pink. Try filling them with strawberry cream yoghurt and sprinkling with hundreds and thousands for children's birthdays...

TIP 3: If you don't have a baking tray, you can take cardboard and wrap it in two layers of aluminium foil. Don't forget to grease your new tray

VARIATIONS
FOR YOUR CORNETS

These tasty little holders can take more than just your run of the mill ice cream and sorbets: why not try using a piping bag filled with creams or other mixtures? You can use different forms for piping, too, such as a star-shaped cover, to make your cornets special!

Mousse au chocolat, white or milk/dark
Single whipped cream
Quark-mousse
Soft cheese and berries (roughly chopped for a lumpy mixture)
(try strawberries, raspberries, blueberries, blackberries, etc)
Creamy soft cheese mixture with plum jam
Mascarpone-creme with Amaretto
Crème patissière with chocolate flakes, orange or coffee liqueur with chopped nuts

CRISPY CROQUANT

250g brown sugar
2 tbs water
100g roughly chopped pistachio nuts

Use a well-sized saucepan to heat the sugar and water on a medium hob. Keep heating until the sugar is dissolved and the sugar begins to caramelise. Add in the chopped pistachios, stir, and quickly pour the mixture out onto an oiled baking tray in thin lines. Leave to cool and then remove from the tray.

For experts, great to prepare in advance
Cooking time: 30 mins.
Serves four

TIP 1: You can also use white sugar for this recipe

TIP 2: Pistachios can be replaced by walnuts, pecans, or hazelnuts

TIP 3: Watch out: the sugar will burn quickly, so do not set your hob too high. It is far better to work with less heat than to end up with burnt sugar! Do not leave the hob, or try to do something else at the same time. And work fast!